The SOUND
A MAN'S KRYPTONITE

LARRY JACKSON

The Sound: A Man's Kryptonite

Copyright © 2019 Larry Jackson

Website:

The following abbreviations are used to identify versions of the Bible used in this book:

Nouns and pronouns referring to deity are capitalized throughout the text of this book unless they are included within a direct quotation, in which case the original capitalization is retained.

Printed in the United States of America
April 2019

ISBN-13: 978-1-7329229-0-7

Breastplate Prayer Publications

Likewise, ye wives,

be in subjection to your own husbands; that, if any obey not the word, they also may without the word be won by the conversation of the wives; While they behold your chaste conversation coupled with fear. Whose adorning let it not be that outward adorning of plaiting the hair, and of wearing of gold, or of putting on of apparel;

But let it be the hidden man of the heart, in that which is not corruptible, even the ornament of a meek and quiet spirit, which is in the sight of God of great price.

—1 Peter 3:1-4

Contents

Chapter 1.   The Kryptonite Effect   5

Chapter 2.   The Sound of the Lord God   21

Chapter 3.   The Sound of a Help Meet   35

Chapter 4.   The Sound of Submission   45

Chapter 5.   The Sound of Influence   59

Chapter 6.   The Sound of Insight   67

Chapter 7.   The Sound of Silence   77

Chapter 8.   The Sound of Seduction   89

Chapter 9.   The Sound of Deception   103

Chapter 10. The Sound That He Listens For   109

Chapter 11. I'm Never Going Back   121

Chapter 12. Bring On the Joy!   135

THE SOUND: A MAN'S KRYPTONITE

For so long women have looked for ways to better connect with the men in their lives and they've had the power all this time, it's the Kryptonite effect!

—*Bishop Larry Jackson*

CHAPTER 1. THE KRYPTONITE EFFECT

CHAPTER 1

The Kryptonite Effect

"The way to a man's heart is through his stomach."
—Fanny Fern (1872)

Fanny Fern wrote the famous phrase *"The way to a man's heart is through his stomach"* when she was a newspaper columnist for the *New York Ledger* in the late 1800s. Ever since then, women have followed her advice. However, nothing could be further from the truth!

Women have been so convinced that a man's heart and food are connected that they will work for hours to cook and cook and cook and win a guy who will eat almost everything in sight and then fall asleep, never getting any closer to her in his heart.

Until he hears The Sound, he probably won't connect with her at the deep emotional level that she needs.

Introducing *The Sound*

This book is designed to challenge ingrained attitudes in women about their relationships with men and introduce them to a time-tested principle that works with the majority of men.

The principle I am speaking about I call *The Sound.*

When the women who come to our *The True Value of a Woman* conferences find out that a man's heart is connected to his ears much more than to his stomach, they are totally surprised. They have never heard about *The Sound.*

That Ain't Fair!

Here is a little personal background about *The Sound.*

When my wife Joanndra and I first got married, we didn't always communicate the way we do now. In fact, we had gotten into the middle of a heated discussion when all of a sudden she stopped talking and changed the tone of her voice. Poof! All the air went out of my frustration. I lost all power to win my point. I said to her, *"That ain't fair!"*

I heard *The Sound*

To this day, she still remembers that moment because of my response. Everything changed. I knew I couldn't fight with her any more. It was years before either of us understood what happened *because I had heard The Sound.*

My wife is actually responsible for the publication of this book. For months I gave her reasons why I didn't want to write my previous book that this one came from, *The True Value of a Woman*. Eventually her gentle but consistent nudging overcame my resistance and, as they say, the rest is history.

Joanndra believed that my first book would help women understand God's purpose for their lives and that they would share its principles with other women who also needed to understand their true value.

She knew they would see that God designed them to be valuable people and they should expect the men in their lives to value and appreciate them, too. That is exactly what happened. It even launched a *The True Value of a Woman* movement, and now she is standing as one with me through the publication of this next book, *The Sound*.

My wife's background was nothing like mine. When we got married, even though I was an elder in the church, educated, and teaching in a technical school, before we met I had grown up in Church Hill, an inner-city neighborhood in Richmond, Virginia. When you grow up on the streets, you don't learn a lot about how to relate properly to a woman, especially someone who would want to stay with you for the rest of her life. I had a lot to learn.

I needed the right mentors and the right woman to help teach me how to love and care for the woman in my life. This understanding also provided principles that I was able to share with other men in churches and conferences.

Men can be takers but they crave *The Sound*

Human nature has embedded deep within each of us a desire to be a taker. It's all about me, without giving back. We will follow the path of least resistance to get what we want. Men have perfected those desires. A woman needs to understand this so she doesn't get frustrated and fight back. Instead, she becomes willing for God to use her to encourage him and build him up.

That day of our heated discussion, when my wife was able to use *The Sound,* she had the ability to position herself on my team by what she said, even in the midst of a disagreement.

God has wired a man's brain to crave *The Sound,* and he can't hear it enough. I am no exception. Men guard this secret about their weakness for *The Sound*, and some have even pleaded with me not to talk about it openly! However, this communication tool is too important to keep hidden. Marriages can be changed as well as father-daughter relationships, mother-son, sister-brother, and co-workers and friends. Men can become stronger toward the things of God.

That's why I have decided to share the principles of *The Sound* in this book. They have worked not only for us but also for many other relationships that have been saved and strengthened using these truths for more than 25 years.

A woman's words of affirmation and encouragement are ear candy to a man when they come from a sincere heart. He has no real defense against it. Even when he has full knowledge that she is using *The Sound*, he is helpless when she does it right.

That's why I call *The Sound* "A Man's Kryptonite."

A Man's Kryptonite

I believe one of the things that will motivate women to purchase this book will be the subtitle *A Man's Kryptonite*. So let's start by understanding Kryptonite, a substance that was invented by the author of the Superman stories. If you have ever read Superman comics or watched Superman cartoons or a Superman movie, you know about Kryptonite. It's a fictitious, crystal-type material, usually green in color, that emits radiation and causes Superman, the Man of Steel, to become weak and sickly. Villains such as the fictional Lex Luthor can defeat Superman's powers with Kryptonite. Enemies who never had a chance to beat Superman now become his equal and even dominate him because of the disabling effects of Kryptonite.

When I compare *The Sound* to the effect of Kryptonite on Superman, I give it a positive context.

The Sound gives a woman the ability to weaken a man's resistance and self-centered pride to turn him toward her, loving her from his heart. He becomes open to an emotional connection to her for life. He becomes stronger toward the things of God. He can be sparked to rise to a new level of responsibility.

God has placed within women the unique ability to improve almost any man with *The Sound*. The responsibility for their relationship doesn't rest on the woman alone, but once she uses *The Sound,* it doesn't matter who is responsible. *Once he hears The Sound*, he will do whatever he can to hear that sound again.

The fictional character of Alexander Joseph "Lex" Luther in the Superman stories is a brilliant, wealthy inventor. Once he realizes the effect Kryptonite has on Superman, his entire focus moves away from direct actions against Superman to acquiring the Kryptonite crystals. He knows he will have the upper hand if he can use Kryptonite against the Man of Steel.

The Sound has a Kryptonite effect on most men, even if the man has not responded to anything else his wife or the woman closest to him has tried to do. *The Sound* helps resolve the disconnect between a man and woman and reconnect him to her out of the emotional center of his being.

In my estimation, the disconnect between a man and his woman has everything to do with him and not her, but this book is not written to men and it is not dealing with men's ingrained attitudes, so let's move forward.

Women Need a New Focus

Armed with the secret weapon of *The Sound,* women should become as focused on using it on their man as Lex Luther was on using Kryptonite for Superman, but for different reasons.

A woman needs to diligently pursue *The Sound* so she can make her man strong, not weak, but first she has to weaken his inhibitions against forming a real relationship. She has to overcome his resistance against becoming vulnerable and entering into a lifelong relationship with her.

A man tends to build a wall between him and a woman, but when that wall is weakened he can become strong for life if she is the woman God has sent to him. Ungodly women use *The Sound,* too, as we shall see, but women who use *The Sound* from pure motives recall the best examples of women in the Bible.

Women can help men more than they can help themselves

For 25 years, I have stood in front of hundreds of thousands of men at men's conferences for Promise Keepers, Men at the Cross, Iron Sharpens Iron, Frontliners, and other men's organizations to try to help them deal with their man-issues. However, once I started *The True Value of a Woman* conferences, I discovered that women are in a much better position to help men with their man-issues than men are themselves. Life-altering changes begin in a man when he meets the woman God has chosen for him if she has the right motives and understands *The Sound.*

Before marriage, few men have a desire to attend premarital workshops or conferences. They are usually happy to leave things alone if there's no apparent conflict. They would rather function with on-the-job training than think in advance about how to improve their relationship with the woman in their lives. This book is not for them. A lot of them just don't get it, anyway.

Studying The Way He Shows His Emotions

Men are experts at putting on a facade when it comes to expressing their emotions to a woman. Although women usually show their emotions, men try to control their emotions or even hold them back entirely. Therefore, it becomes essential for a woman to study a man so she can spot subtle signs of his emotional connectedness to her. Once she knows the clues, she will be able to avoid having a spirit of resentment toward him and the fear that she is giving out more than she is getting back.

This knowledge is vital for the woman who is dealing with the unemotional man.

Some men seem bankrupt when it comes to sharing love and affection toward the women in their lives. Let me assure you, he isn't bankrupt. He is using a different currency. When you love this kind of man, you have to learn his unspoken body language so that you will hold back from complaining and correcting him.

A woman needs to study a man's style to discover what he enjoys doing. When she takes the time to study his favorite team or examine his hobbies, she gains the ability to pose intelligent questions and make insightful statements during a conversation.

Men have no problem getting excited about sports. When your unemotional man gets around other men who are discussing something that interests them, excitement is all over his face, but most men will never express their feelings to a woman at the same level. I guarantee he feels joy toward you and enjoys being joyful as much as you do, so don't be overtaken if he doesn't outwardly show a wide range of emotions of love and joy.

If you watch your man when he is around other men, sometimes you can discover more about how much he appreciates the life and relationship he shares with you than when you are alone together. That seems odd, doesn't it? But because of a man's competitive nature, it makes him feel good when the woman in his life treats him better than women treat his friends or associates in his circle.

Even though you have a deep need in your own heart to hear his words of affirmation and love, don't overlook or dismiss his subtle actions that communicate his love. He will look at you across a crowded room with a wink or a look of pleasure and love on his face. His smile will be a true sign of his joy and happiness with you. Sometimes you will only find him out because someone in his circles tells you how much he talks about you. Learn to recognize and even celebrate his little attempts to express his emotions to you concerning your relationship.

Become Interested In His Hobbies

Take football for example. If you do not understand much about a sport that he loves, go online to YouTube and look at a video on the subject. Find the five-minute video on understanding football that discusses vocabulary, player positions, scoring and much more. This research will only take five minutes of your time, but the insight into your man will be worth it. View the video until you can easily follow the narrator's explanations. Then and only then should you attempt to discuss football with your man. You can even use this to successfully draw some of his attention away from his male friends! Moreover, if you become a fan of his team that will be even better!

Golf is another example. I've taught women in less than five minutes how to understand and score the game of golf. Once you follow the game, intelligent conversation can be another way to connect with him while he is watching a tournament.

Also, men who enjoy video games (gamers) love to have the women in their lives capable of handling a controller. Instead of losing his attention because he constantly brings over friends who take his time away from you, he can play with you instead. You can even play online together at times when you are apart.

Remember, *when he hears The Sound,* he will hear your heart speaking and not just your words. Always remember that men have no defense against *The Sound.*

Always Be Enthusiastic About His Small Gifts

Some men understand that it is safe to speak of his love to a woman directly, but other men avoid direct expressions of love and choose to show love by acts of service or purchasing gifts. If you learn to interpret these acts of service and gifts correctly, you will see that they are unspoken signs of his affection and a reaffirmation of how much he values you.

> *Please, please, never push your man away or make him feel that the things he does to help you or the small gifts he brings do not matter to you. If you do, the door will shut fast, and it will be difficult to get it open again.*

All people have things they like and don't like. Women are much different from men and even from one another other. Some women like gifts, others like being served, and others like words of affirmation. Most men have a default switch set to performance. He thinks the woman in his life will recognize and respond to his *performance.* If the woman is looking for something else, his innocent attempt to please her could become contentious.

While he is preparing or purchasing a gift, he is visualizing how it would make the woman happy and how she would lavish him with praise and gratefulness. If he seems to do everything wrong, understand that *he does everything to hear The Sound.* When you realize this fact, you will not miss opportunities to use *The Sound* to become connected to him in his heart.

He can be trained to give you exactly what you desire, but you must allow him to start first. It is difficult to push an elephant, but an elephant that is walking can be guided perfectly.

One caution—Don't look for too much, too soon.

NOTES

THE SOUND: A MAN'S KRYPTONITE

The voice of the LORD is powerful; the voice of the LORD is majestic.

—Psalms 29:4

Chapter 2
The Sound of the LORD God

"And they heard the sound of the LORD God
walking in the garden in the cool of the day."
—*Genesis 3:8 ESV*

Before you can fully appreciate your man's heart to give to you and why you should respond with gratitude, go back to Genesis to understand *The Sound of the Lord God* Who created us. An understanding of human nature according to creative order can give you a true, balanced foundation for a lifelong relationship.

The creation account in Genesis chapters 1 and 2 leaves no doubt that everything on earth had an original design and a creative order. This is especially evident in God's creation of the man and woman who would receive from Him the responsibility of oversight and stewardship of the earth, beginning in the Garden of Eden. The Bible lets us listen in on *The Sound of the Lord's Creation* and *The Sound of the Lord's Correction*.

The Sound of the Lord's Creation

The first chapter of Genesis lets us listen in on *The Sound of the Lord's Creation* as He created man in His own image and likeness, male and female.

"And God said, Let us make man in our image, after our likeness: and let them have dominion over the fish of the sea, and over the fowl of the air, and over the cattle, and over all the earth, and over every creeping thing that creepeth upon the earth.

"So God created man in his own image, in the image of God created he him; male and female created he them"
—Genesis 1:26-27

God gave them a beautiful place to live

Think for a moment about the most beautiful place that you have ever seen. Now think about the fact that the Garden of Eden would make that beautiful place seem like a dump by comparison. Before man was created, God had prepared a place for humanity that only heaven could top, and He placed the man and woman in it to enjoy the beauty of His creation.

The first couple enjoyed evening walks and talks with the Godhead, having unimaginable conversations. All of the animals on the entire earth were in complete harmony with mankind and with one another. There was no death anywhere on the whole planet. It never rained; there were no storms or hurricanes, no cold or snow, no earthquakes, no wildfires or any such thing. Nothing but beauty as far as the eyes could see.

One thing in creation was "not good"

In the creation account, the only time the phrase "not good" was used concerned the fact that the man was alone.

> *"And the LORD God said, It is not good that the man should be alone; I will make him an help meet for him."*
> *—Genesis 2:18*

Before the woman's creation, God instructed the man to search the animals and give them names. The man wasn't looking for an animal to be his mate, since that would have been outside of creative order, He was looking for someone like himself who could join him in fellowship so they could worship God together.

> *"And out of the ground the LORD God formed every beast of the field, and every fowl of the air; and brought them unto Adam to see what he would call them: and whatsoever Adam called every living creature, that was the name thereof.*
> *"And Adam gave names to all cattle, and to the fowl of the air, and to every beast of the field; but for Adam there was not found an help meet for him."*
> *—Genesis 2:19-20*

Adam fulfilled his assignment. Not a single animal was a suitable help meet for Adam, so he was still alone. However, he was not complaining. He lacked a mate, but he never asked God to give him one.

God gave the man a gift—a woman

Providing a woman for the man was God's idea, not the man's. When the man couldn't find anyone who fit the job description as a suitable mate, the time had come for the woman to be created and brought forth. The *fact* of the woman's creation was not a surprise to the man, only *how and when* it happened.

The Council of God decided it was not good for man to function alone and worship alone in his relationship with the Godhead. God declared that it was time for the man to have a relationship with a woman, so He decided to create a woman for the man from the man's own side. As a result, the man and woman were connected under God from the time of creation.

> *"And Adam said, This is now bone of my bones, and flesh of my flesh: she shall be called Woman, because she was taken out of Man."*
> *—Genesis 2:23*

As the first couple, the man and woman had common authority over everything God created, except for one another. In God's original design, the woman was connected to her husband in worship, authority, and blessings. Together they enjoyed their union and worship experience with God.

Divine blessing on mating of the man and woman

Even before the man and woman's physical creation, God instructed them to be fruitful and multiply, making it clear that they would mate.

> *"And God blessed them, and God said unto them, Be fruitful, and multiply, and replenish the earth."*
> *—Genesis 1:28*

It is important to note that the creation of the woman wasn't just for mating purposes. In Chapter 3 we will explore her purpose, but suffice it to say their full attention focused on the Godhead and exercising dominion over the earth.

The Sound of the Lord's Correction

God gave Adam one commandment—Do not eat from the tree in the midst of the Garden, which He identified as the Tree of the Knowledge of Good and Evil. It was the only thing forbidden to Adam and his wife. Since everything on the planet was under their complete control, there was no need for

Adam and his wife to exercise their wills to demonstrate obedience to God in any other area.

God's rule forbidding access to this one tree gave the man the opportunity to exercise his unique God-given will by choosing to obey God, but he blew it. He failed the test. Here is how it happened. The man and woman had a common enemy, embodied in a snake. This enemy beguiled the woman so that she took fruit from the Tree of the Knowledge of Good and Evil and gave it to her husband, who was there witnessing this entire interaction.

> "... she took of the fruit thereof, and did eat, and gave also unto her husband with her; and he did eat. And the eyes of them both were opened, and they knew that they were naked."
> —Genesis 3:6-7

Disrupted gender roles and separation from God

God created man as giver and woman as receiver. When the woman gave the fruit to her husband and he ate, that was a disregard for the gender roles of God's creative order. The serpent contradicted God and then the woman became the giver and the man became the receiver. This was the opposite of creative order.

- Man was created to be a giver, but became a receiver.

THE SOUND: A MAN'S KRYPTONITE

- Woman was created to be a receiver, but became a giver.

When the man and woman disobeyed God, they lost the precious gift of fellowship with Him. There was a new sound in the Garden—*The Sound of the Lord God's Correction.* When God levied curses on everyone involved, He made it clear that the woman was not the primary source of the sin problem. However, her influence cannot be overlooked. The man had a relationship with God before the woman was created, and he had heard *The Sound of the Lord God.* Yet she was able to persuade the man to disobey a direct commandment from God. That was some power.

The Bible does not record what the woman said to the man to persuade him to eat, but *when he heard The Sound* from the woman it moved his heart to have regard for her *Sound* and to have disregard for *The Sound of the Lord God.*

> *"And they heard the sound of the Lord God walking in the garden in the cool of the day, and the man and his wife hid themselves from the presence of the Lord God among the trees of the garden. But the Lord God called to the man and said to him, 'Where are you?'*
> *"And he said, 'I heard the sound of you in the garden, and I was afraid, because I was naked, and I hid myself.'*

27

"He said, 'Who told you that you were naked?
Have you eaten of the tree of which I
commanded you not to eat?'
"The man said, 'The woman whom you gave
to be with me, she gave me fruit of the tree,
and I ate.'
"Then the Lord God said to the woman,
'What is this that you have done?'
"The woman said, 'The serpent deceived me,
and I ate.'"
—Genesis 3:8-13 ESV.

Adam was perfect with no weaknesses, but *when he heard The Sound* from his wife she convinced him to go against God. The power of this woman over her husband baffles the mind. I believe that is why part of the curse that was placed upon her was to be subject to her husband.

All-Out Assault on Masculinity Today

An all-out assault on masculinity over the last 20 years is starting to bear bad fruit in the lives of men. It is of great importance to help men to once again embrace their roles in society as men as God gave it to them at creation. Women must realize that they will benefit when gender roles are once again clearly defined as they were at creation. They should fight against progressives who want to annihilate masculinity. Restructuring men as hairy women leaves a significant vacuum that will cause more problems than anyone has considered, as Jack Myers writes in *The Future of Men: Masculinity in the Twenty-First Century.*

What happens when men return to giving

There is no evidence that the God-given desire for man to be a giver has changed. However, there is evidence that he is suppressing that desire because so many women have taken his role and most men choose the path of least resistance. I am aware that some men aren't suppressing their desire to give. They are devoid of the understanding and motivation to be the giver in their relationships. This fact doesn't change the fact that he was designed to give and when he functions in his God-given role, everything inside of him is energized with excitement.

God told the man to give the woman the ultimate thing he possesses, his life! The man who embraces this truth and releases his life for the woman in his life will experience the greatest joy he has ever known. After that, everything else is easy. The Bible says:

> *"So ought men to love their wives as their own bodies. He that loveth his wife loveth himself. For no man ever yet hated his own flesh; but nourisheth and cherisheth it, even as the Lord the church: For we are members of his body, of his flesh, and of his bones. For*

this cause shall a man leave his father and
mother, and shall be joined unto his wife, and
they two shall be one flesh."
—*Ephesians 5:28-31*

Start watching as men recover their masculinity according to the creative model and once again become the source for whatever anyone else is receiving—especially the females in their lives. His face and eyes will light up. His shoulders will straighten. He will be carefully observing to see if she is impressed. This attitude might be viewed as pride, and for some it is, but most of the time it is a man enjoying being a man and pleasing the woman in his life. I believe *The Sound* will spark in men an initiative that is now lying dormant—their God-given purpose to be providers.

NOTES

Chapter 3. The Sound of a Help Meet

"Love is a fruit in season at all times, and is within the reach of every hand."
—*Mother Teresa*

Chapter 3. The Sound of a Help Meet

Chapter 3

The Sound of a Help Meet

"And the LORD God said, It is not good that the man should be alone; I will make him an help meet for him."
—Genesis 2:18

When God defined the woman He had created, He called her a "help meet" (KJV) for the man. She was not a "help mate," as it says in other translations. It is essential to discover the difference between the two.

Ezer and *Neged*—Hebrew Words for "Help" and "Meet"

In my book *The True Value of Woman*, I explain the meanings of the Hebrew words *ezer* and *neged,*[1] which are translated "help" and "meet" in Genesis 2:18 (KJV). The Hebrew words *ezer* and *neged* make up the phrase used to describe the woman God brought to Adam—"help meet."

Ezer is a Hebrew verb translated "help."

Neged, is an adverb translated "meet." It modifies the word help. It means in front of, in sight of, conspicuous, straightforward.

---

[1] *Strong's Concordance* number H5048.

This chapter is about the woman's vital role to help a man and how she helps him. Our focus is on the Hebrew word *neged*, translated "meet." As you will see, these definitions have nothing to do with mating, which is a separate topic. This is about *The True Value of a Woman* and how she contributes to their relationship.

Why is the woman in front? What is she saying?

According to the Hebrew words *ezer* and *neged*, a help meet would be in front, but what would she be doing there?

Uses of the Hebrew word *neged, translated "meet" (KJV)*

- What is conspicuous, what is in front of
- In front of, straightforward, before, in sight of
- In front of oneself, straightforward
- Before your face, in your view or purpose
- What is in front of, corresponding to
- In front of, before
- In the sight or presence of
- Parallel to
- Over, for
- In front, opposite
- At a distance
- From the front of, away from

- From before the eyes of, opposite to, at a distance from
- From before, in front of
- As far as the front of

Uses of the Hebrew word *nagad,* root word of *neged* (meet)

Let's study the word *neged* a little deeper. *Neged* comes from the Hebrew root word *nagad.* Here are some uses of *nagad.*

- To be conspicuous, tell, make known
- To tell, declare
- To tell, announce, report
- To declare, make known, expound
- To inform of
- To publish, declare, proclaim
- To avow, acknowledge, confess
- Messenger (participle)
- To be told, be announced, be reported

God had a high purpose when He created the woman as a help meet. Notice the emphasis of being in front of and not behind.

When I present this list to women in my *The True Value of a Woman* conferences, they are shocked. This list implies that woman was created to be in front of the man. Notice, it doesn't say she was created to lead the man. There is a difference.

Nagad has to do with speaking and *neged* means to be out in front. God created a helper who would be out in front of the man speaking, making proclamations. What is she proclaiming? Let's look at the passage in Genesis 2 again to get a true understanding.

> *"And the LORD God said, It is not good that the man should be alone; I will make him an help meet for him."*
> —*Genesis 2:18 KJV*

God brought a woman to the man so that he would not be alone. Metaphorically, a woman is in a position and attitude that a man has a tough time resisting, even when he is fully aware of what is taking place. We understand from the Hebrew words *nagad* and *neged* that God did not instruct the woman to physically or symbolically stand behind a man. However, He did not say she should stand in front of the man and lead by facing forward, either.

You get up in front with a man by asking about his vision

Before a woman can understand her correct positional attitude in relation to her man, as God has declared it, she has to ask him questions to understand his vision and purpose. She can't understand his vision and purpose and the vehicles he will use to accomplish them—and join him in his vision—until she asks.

She needs to ask him questions about his vision in a non-threatening way, with *The Sound*. That is how she communicates honestly that she is only asking questions because she is on his side. He can tell that she loves him and wants to be vitally involved in the pursuit and accomplishment of his goals and vision.

According to their creative purpose together, the woman is in complete oneness with the man and his vision when she joins him in his worship of God. They worship Father God together and speak to the generation about His greatness and His purpose for humanity. That position is similar to the Church today in its relationship with Jesus (the Bride of Christ) in the earth. The Bride of Christ stays out in front announcing His goodness, His coming, and His greatness. Likewise, the woman, the bride of the man, accomplishes this purpose for her husband relationally.

A woman willing to initially take responsibility for her relationship with the man can make him successful even when he neglects his responsibility for the relationship. She stays hopeful that one day he will change *when he hears The Sound*. He will see the significance of taking responsibility for it himself.

How to ask questions with *The Sound of a Help Meet*

Most men need time to process information and usually perform this task through quiet reflection or being alone. Women don't have this problem because they can communicate with both sides of their brain at the same time. Women who expect men to process information in the same way as they do could become frustrated and could create conflict.

Instead, let him hear *The Sound* coming from you by your kind words and gestures that show consideration of your man's different way of doing things. That can make a great deal of difference in your relationship.

When he hears The Sound, he will listen more closely to your questions and his actions will be designed to keep you happy. Positive results never become a reality with the wrong approach in words or tone. Never talk down to a man as though he is ignorant, even if he is. Never pressure him to give immediate answers, based on your timetable. *Always remember The Sound.*

This may be difficult to remember at times due to his actions or lack thereof, but he really wants to please you!

NOTES

"This attitude of complete submission and
complete trust is of course the key to working out
our own salvation in fear and trembling and is
the mark of a truly spiritual Christian."
—*John F. Walvoord*

CHAPTER 4. THE SOUND OF SUBMISSION

Chapter 4

The Sound of Submission

*"But the meek shall inherit the earth; and
shall delight themselves in the abundance of
peace."*
—Psalms 37:11

Some of the most significant dialogs in *The
True Value of a Woman* Marriage Seminars concern
how to function during a disagreement without
facing down the person in a negative way. When a
woman has the God-given sensitivity to stay in a
position of meekness, peace, and submission to her
man, she is empowered to not only agree but also
disagree while keeping the right spirit.

Sarah understood *the Sound of Submission*
when speaking to her husband Abraham, but
unfortunately she misused it and persuaded him to
stand against God.

Abram was a very wealthy man living in Ur
of the Chaldees when God told him to leave his
home and go to a city that He would show him. God
didn't give him any specific geographical directions
or destination, but He promised a blessing if he
obeyed.

*"Now the LORD had said unto Abram, Get
thee out of thy country, and from thy kindred,*

*and from thy father's house, unto a land that I
will shew thee: And I will make of thee a great
nation, and I will bless thee, and make thy
name great; and thou shalt be a blessing: And
I will bless them that bless thee, and curse him
that curseth thee: and in thee shall all families
of the earth be blessed."*
—*Genesis 12:1-3*

Abram's wife willingly followed him, and
they set out with his father Terah and nephew Lot,
who also had great wealth.

Sarah kept submitting until she wanted something

Not many women today would start packing,
but Sarah did! She instructed her handmaids to pack
their possessions in preparation to wander. Think
about a husband coming home from work to inform
his wife that they had to move, but he didn't know
where they were going or even in what direction.
Well, most women may be accustomed to not
knowing the direction a man is traveling, but I
digress.

God had established a covenant with Abram
and God's blessing came through his obedience.
Eventually Abram and Lot's wealth was so great
that they couldn't dwell together comfortably any
more in the same region. Abram told Lot to choose

where he wanted to reside and he would go in the other direction. Lot chose the fertile land near Sodom and Gomorrah.

At this point, God changed Abram's name to Abraham and changed his wife's name from Sari to Sarah.

Now think about this one. A husband comes home and tells his wife that her name has changed and she has a new name. Sarah accepts her new name and keeps moving across the earth with no idea where she is going.

Abraham then tells Sarah to lie to a king and say that she is his sister instead of his wife. He is worried that the king will kill him to take Sarah for himself. She obeys him and lies to the king, and the king does take her as one of his wives. God rescues her from the king and delivers her back into Abraham's care.

After these adventures, God tells Abraham that he will have a son in his old age through his wife Sarah. She is long past childbearing years and more significant than that, she is also barren. Sarah hears it because she is standing in the tent door. She starts laughing that anything so ridiculous could happen.

Although she has followed her husband to this point, seemingly through thick and thin, this was where she breaks ranks and takes matters into her own hands. Sarah comes up with a plan of her own. She tells Abraham her interpretation of what God meant and what Abraham should do.

Remember, Abraham had obeyed God, left his homeland and family, and wandered on the earth, looking for a city without knowing the destination. He had received the promise from God that he would be the father of nations in his old age. He had seen God protect his wife from a king, and much more. Yet when Sarah introduced her plan, he listened to his wife instead of God! He went against the word of the Lord to fulfill the word of his wife.

This woman had real power. How did she do it? The Apostle Peter gives us a clue in his first epistle.

> *"Even as Sarah obeyed Abraham, calling him lord: whose daughters ye are, as long as ye do well, and are not afraid with any amazement."*
> *—1 Peter 3:6*

Did you see that? She was "calling him lord"! Abraham was no match for *The Sound of Submission* from his wife. Even a man with a direct word from God has a difficult time competing with *The Sound*.

Where Submission Came From

God didn't create humans to be subservient to one another. It was only after the disobedience of the

48

first couple that God pronounced a curse upon both the man and woman and subjection came to bear:

- The man had to work hard forever to produce for himself and his family.
- The woman would bear children in sorrow and be subservient to the man.

> *"Unto the woman he said, I will greatly multiply thy sorrow and thy conception; in sorrow thou shalt bring forth children; and thy desire [longing] shall be to thy husband, and he shall rule over thee."*
> *—Genesis 3:16*

The word "rule" in this verse is the Hebrew word *mashal*. The definition of *mashal* is "to govern." Governance is elected or appointed. It is only a dictatorship when governance is seized.

When the man and woman were created, neither one had the rule over the other. They were explicitly designed to be one and function as one. They were not even described as "equal," since that mindset would have made them two separate beings. They were one!

Why Submission Works

Some wives reject submission in marriage when their husband wants to lead because they think they will lose their uniqueness. However, the opposite is usually true. I've met women who work in the corporate world, run businesses, function in ministry, yet have embraced the submissive, out-in-front principle to oversee their homes and are some of the most unique people I've met.

You cannot understand why submission works at home outside of the Word of God. You have to renew your mind first by embracing and applying God's Word! Some people use other methods to try to understand relationships, but in the life of a believer the Bible is absolutely the best tool. *The Sound of Submission* takes practice but it is an effective weapon to eliminate conflict at home. Biblical submission is not weak. It is the essence of persuasive power.

When a wife is forward-looking in mindset and practice, the benefits of her position and attitude increase daily!

When a woman is a true help meet, she helps make the family's relational goals and purpose become a reality. It is time for Christian women to return to functioning in the family based on their God-given design. Become that woman!

Why "In Your Face" Doesn't Work with a Man

When a woman positions herself wrong during a disagreement or even a regular discussion and gets in a man's face, she hasn't thought through what logical response to expect from him. When she faces him down, she forces him to defend his position and protect himself as a warrior. Then no one wins. The whole family is in disarray.

When you confront a man, hormones like adrenalin, vasopressin and testosterone are released that cause him to react with a fight-or-flight response.

But when he hears The Sound, he will not fight or flee. He will respond to the challenge intelligently because you have made him aware of the issues with *the Sound of Submission.*

Hormones released in the right way cause him to produce, protect and provide (P3) for his woman and if he is married his wife and family! Being alert and prepared to use The Sound of Submission makes all the difference in the relationship.

When he hears The Sound of his woman acknowledging that he has performed well in some area, excitement explodes in his heart and his desire to hear those words again becomes his new focus. Testosterone skyrockets in a man whose woman is pleased and grateful for what he does.

Cleaving to Pursue You Again

The longer a couple has lived together in marriage, the more they might take one another for granted. In Genesis we see this vital relational clue:

"Therefore shall a man leave his father and his mother, and shall cleave unto his wife: and they shall be one flesh."
—*Genesis 2:24*

The Hebrew word for cleave is *dâbaq* (daw-bak'). Here are the meanings:

- to impinge
- to cling or adhere
- to catch by pursuit
- to abide, fast, cleave (fast together)
- follow hard after
- to stay close
- be joined together
- overtake, pursue

Those definitions sound more like a boyfriend/girlfriend relationship than a husband/wife. Not many husbands still actively pursue their wives. Women say that their men no longer express their love and desire for them.

Making some adjustments to build more excitement

However, all of this can change with just a few adjustments by the woman. I hear some of you asking the question, *"What about him?"* Remember, men love the path of least resistance. If he can get by without cleaving, he absolutely will. But, once his wife becomes more flirty and playful, he will usually respond. Don't just drop hints. Let him know what you want and he will give you what you desire. Make him think about you all day while he is away.

There is a great commercial by one of the major phone carriers demonstrating this principle. The husband is leaving for a trip and his taxi is waiting. When he hugs his children and his wife, she gives him a note that the kids have written and she tells him that he should read it on the plan. After he enters the taxi, she comes to the car door and hands him another note. This one is from her and she tells him that she *doesn't* recommend he read it on the plan. This causes him to look at her and the taxi driver with excitement! This woman understands how to keep him thinking about her, even while he is away. When a woman does this correctly, it upsets the status quo and injects new energy into the relationship.

When marriages have little or no intimacy, erectile dysfunction can become a medical concern, and there may be some truth to this fact, but I think another issue is too often overlooked. Men are very simple creatures. When a woman makes herself available and accessible to him, exciting things begin to happen!

A man loves to think about his woman, but what is he thinking when he thinks about you? Does he have to fight through your negativity, complaints, or even your worries to have pleasant thoughts about you as his woman?

NOTES

CHAPTER 5. THE SOUND OF INFLUENCE

One of the best ways to influence people is to make them feel important.

—Roy T. Bennett

Chapter 5

The Sound of Influence

"A gracious woman gains respect."
—Proverbs 11:16

When a fish gets caught, it fights for its life to get off the hook or the net. The water turns violent with resistance. This violence excites the fisherman because he knows that the fish is almost in the boat!

A woman who understands *The Sound of Influence* should have the same mindset as that fisherman. When she sees her man in the throes of resistance, she should stay the course, continue to pray, and believe that her catch will soon be secured.

Since her goal is strengthening their relationship, his resistance does not weaken her resolve. She knows that her man gets strengthened by taking a defensive posture. That does not indicate her failure but means that success is near.

"The wise woman builds her house."
—Proverbs 14:1

God designed women for greatness. Wise women can have undeniable influence on the men in their lives and even society. God did not remove a woman's ability to move a man's heart with *The Sound*, even after the Fall.

Encouragement Gives *The Sound of Influence*

I hear a common criticism from women that men don't listen. They lament, "I've told him over and over again, and he still doesn't get it!"

I respond to those women, "Stop *telling* him and start *encouraging* him."

Usually they give me a blank look and ask, "Now how would I do that?"

And I answer, *"Remember The Sound."* When a man doesn't seem to listen, don't give up. Remember that his ears and his heart are connected.

When you need something done, don't nag. Remember the saying, "You get more with honey than you do with vinegar!"

Tell him how good you feel when he does it. Tell him how you would feel if he did what you desire. Then he will be motivated to start doing it sooner than you expected and he will want to do it over and over again to hear *The Sound.*

Remember, most men are addicted to *The Sound*! They can't hear it enough!

How *The Sound of Influence* Won a War

Prophetess Deborah is the only female judge among the 12 Hebrew judges in the Old Testament. When she told Barak, her military commander, to take 10,000 troops and defeat the Canaanite armies led by Sisera, he said he would do it with one stipulation, if Deborah went with him. She agreed, but she also prophesied that God would deliver Sisera into the hands of a woman.

As the battle unfolded, Sisera and the Canaanites began to lose so Sisera fled for his life on foot. He came to the tent of Jael, a woman mentioned only once in the Bible, and put his trust in her.

Jael is an example of how *"The Sound"* puts a man at ease, even when he is dealing with high levels of stress. In this case, a man was running for his life but he heard *The Sound.*

> *"Turn in . . . to me; fear not. So when he had turned in unto her into the tent, she covered him with a mantle."*
> —*Judges 4:18*

Sisera went trustingly into her tent. It was not just what Jael said, even though he needed a place to hide, but how she said it. Her words made him feel safe and comfortable. When he asked for water, she gave him milk.

We know he felt safe because he asked her to stand in the tent door to watch for anyone who might be searching for him, then send them away. He felt so much at ease with Jael that he fell asleep, even though he knew soldiers were out searching for him and would kill him if they found him.

While Sisera slept, Jael took a giant nail and drove it through his head and killed him. When he was dead, she called to Barak and revealed what she had done. Deborah's prophecy that Sisera would fall into a woman's hands was fulfilled by Jael's brave deed and the victory was complete, all because a woman knew what words to speak to make a soldier vulnerable. She made *The Sound of Influence.*

Unmatched Power of a Woman's Influence

A woman's power is unmatched when she reaches the heart of a man with *The Sound.* It is time for women to use their power in the way that God intended.

Get ready to be empowered to change the world. Learn how to make *The Sound* in the right place at the right time.

A vast majority of women have never known anyone willing to discuss and teach them how to influence the men in their lives. I hope that the women reading this book will not only learn this but also teach other women the principles of *The Sound.*

It is vital for women to prepare for the full range of results and reactions from the men who will be the focus of their initiatives. My apologies to my brethren for revealing these all-important brotherhood secrets that even we very seldom discuss.

Sound of Influence Saves Marriages Biblically

Over the years, I've had the privilege of teaching the principles in this book to couples in our marriage seminars and retreats. Without fail, one or more of the husbands will lament that I'm giving away too much information and putting him at a disadvantage. In my response, I help him to recognize how much he will benefit if his wife understands and embraces this teaching. Then I walk him through several Scripture references to help strengthen my point.

Men are always surprised to find out that the Bible has already revealed secrets of *The Sound* in many places like this one:

> *"A soft answer turneth away wrath: but grievous words stir up anger."*
> —*Proverbs 15:1*

The principle of a soft answer works for anyone who uses it, but when a woman uses a soft answer it explodes with the power of truth. She can make a man smile and become puzzled all at the same time. He smiles because of the way she makes him feel but he is puzzled because she just got him to do something he didn't think he would do. It's all because of *The Sound of Influence.*

NOTES

_____

_____

_____

_____

_____

_____

_____

_____

The goal is to turn data into information, and information into insight.
—Carly Fiorina

Chapter 6

The Sound of Insight

"Abigail . . . hurried and got down from the donkey and fell before David on her face and bowed to the ground. She fell at his feet and said, 'On me alone, my lord, be the guilt. Please let your servant speak in your ears, and hear the words of your servant. Let not my lord regard this worthless fellow, Nabal, for as his name is, so is he. Nabal is his name, and folly is with him.'"
—*1 Samuel 25:23-25 ESV*

A woman named Abigail in the Bible used *The Sound of Insight* to prevent David, the future king of Israel, from making a big mistake that could have disrupted his relationship with God and the whole course of his life.

Abigail was married to a very wealthy man named Nabal. Before David became king, he and his men were living in the wilderness. Wherever they went, they would often protect the property of others nearby.

One of the men who benefited was Nabal. When David heard that Nabal was shearing sheep, he knew it would be appropriate during a time of feasting to send his men to request food. He gave them this message for Nabal: "Please give whatever you can afford to your servants and to your son David."

However, the Bible says that Nabal, Abigail's husband, was a fool. He rejected David's request for food and supplies. David had an army and could have taken it by force, but he had shown mercy on Nabal. That fool completely dismissed him and his men and acted as if he didn't know David.

Provoked to anger, David assembled 400 men to go and utterly destroy Nabal's household. When Abigail heard about Nabal's attitude and David's intentions, she assembled her servants, gathered supplies and food, and met David on the road.

Abigail was a beautiful woman with high intelligence. Because of her wisdom and her understanding and insight, she helped save the lives of many men.

Abigail honored David when she met him. She reminded him that God would make his future dynasty a lasting one. Then she humbly asked him to forgive Nabal and she took the blame on herself.

> *"I pray thee, forgive the trespass of thine handmaid: for the LORD will certainly make my lord a sure house; because my lord fighteth the battles of the LORD, and evil hath not been found in thee all thy days.*
> *—1 Samuel 25:28*

David listened to Abigail because he heard *The Sound of Insight.* Therefore, he turned away from his murderous intentions.

> *"David said to Abigail, 'Blessed be the Lord, the God of Israel, who sent you this day to meet me! Blessed be your discretion, and blessed be you, who have kept me this day from bloodguilt and from working salvation with my own hand! For as surely as the Lord, the God of Israel, lives, who has restrained me from hurting you, unless you had hurried and come to meet me, truly by morning there had not been left to Nabal so much as one male.'"*
> —1 Samuel 25:32-34 ESV

Bishop Wellington Boone wrote in his book *Women Are Kingmakers!* about an additional outcome of *The Sound of Influence* in David's life. After David listened to Abigail and turned away from harming Nabal, he had an opportunity for another life-changing decision. Bishop Boone wrote:

> "David discovered Saul asleep and could have killed him with his own spear and taken the kingdom from Saul by violence right then, but he said, 'I refuse to touch God's anointed.'

"Why? Abigail had already sown into him the kingly quality of not taking his own revenge. God, the One who had called him, was the One who was supposed to put him in the place where he should be. He said, 'God will fight for me. Even though Saul is delivered into my hand, I can still go down even lower because a woman has shown me what I am supposed to be, and the level where I am supposed to walk, because she was a Kingmaker.'"[2]

Nabal died shortly after the encounter with David. Then David took Abigail as his wife, and she was no longer married to a fool but married to a king. Abigail was fit for a king!

The Sound of Insight Works Everywhere

I have seen mothers use *The Sound of Insight* with their sons with a positive response when nothing else has worked. Sisters have seen it work on brothers. Women in the marketplace have found that it works on fellow male coworkers and customers.

God has given some women even greater wisdom and influence than earthly queens. They are His daughters and queens wherever they go.

---

[2] Wellington Boone, *Women Are Kingmakers!* (Virginia Beach, VA: APPTE Publishing, 2019).

Self-Appointed Queens

When a woman wears a shirt with the word "Queen" across the front, she is indicating that she is a Queen and should be treated that way. Both single and married women wear these shirts, but making the proclamation without a King is self appointing. They want the world to know that they have decided to pursue education or focus on a lucrative career, which to them is a better life than marriage. However, remember that a queen without a king lives to be old and alone.

Some women bring an occasional man into their lives from time to time to help them deal with loneliness. They think that will be better than a husband. It might be exciting for a time, but often it is another dead end of loneliness.

I clearly understand that a woman doesn't need a man in her life to be happy and fulfilled. I currently have three unmarried daughters who live very full and happy lives. However, each of my daughters would love to have a husband who is a man of God and would cleave to her as his wife. She can anoint him king and he can anoint her as queen.

Gratitude for Your Husband

Every king knows he isn't complete without a queen whom he can love and for whom he can provide kingdom resources. If you are already married, let your husband know how grateful you are to be his wife. Watch his eyes light up with joy and excitement. You have made his day three times over, and he feels like a king.

The other men in his life will hear that you told him how important he is to you. Without realizing it, he will work harder and create more just because you are secure in his love.

NOTES

CHAPTER 7. THE SOUND OF SILENCE

Silence is a source of Great Strength.

—Lao Tzu

Chapter 7. The Sound of Silence

Chapter 7
The Sound of Silence

"Even fools are thought wise when they keep
silent; with their mouths shut, they seem
intelligent.
—Proverbs 17:28 NLT

Every woman has the opportunity to bless a man with *The Sound of Silence*. Instead of destroying a relationship with her former words and attitudes, she can put to silence negative words and the things that she knows have hurt him in the past. *The Sound of Silence* will gain his attention and encourage his heart.

The Apostle Paul tells us how we can help someone benefit from things that we keep silent about.

"Let no corrupt communication proceed out
of your mouth, but that which is good to the
use of edifying, that it may minister grace
unto the hearers."
—Ephesians 4:29

When a woman learns to use these guidelines to communicate with her man, power is released. When she never says anything corrupt, *The Sound of Silence* makes life better.

Paul said:

"Let your speech be always with grace,
seasoned with salt, that ye may know how ye
ought to answer every man."
—Colossians 4:6

Arguments and Anger

Arguing should be the first thing that goes silent when you practice *The Sound of Silence*. If you feel that you need to argue about something every day, that is a faulty mindset. Scripture can help you get rid of that pattern forever.

Remember the premise that a man's ears are connected to his heart. Therefore, it should come as no surprise to you that in his heart he has a hatred for arguing. When you think you want to argue, try being silent instead. Give your man a blessing.

"It is better to dwell in the corner of the
housetop, than with a brawling woman and in
a wide house."
—Proverbs 25:24

"A foolish child is a father's ruin, and a
quarrelsome wife is like the constant dripping
of a leaky roof."
—Proverbs 19:13

The harder the words from your mouth that fall on his ears, the harder it will be for you to reach his heart. When you argue, a man goes into a competitive, protective zone to get away from you—

the one who is being combative. Never allow him to enter a combat zone where you are the focus of his combat. Take him instead into zones where he attempts to prove his love for you!

"Let the angry word be answered only with a kiss."
—Thomas Hill

"Say what you mean, but don't say it mean."
—Andrew Wachter

Arguments and complaints may appear on the surface to be helping the situation, but they never do.

Women arguing with women.

This fact may shock you, but men even hate hearing a woman argue with another woman. Some TV and reality shows sell the idea of conflicts between women who use offensive language and fight and scheme against one another while wearing little or no clothing. The lack of clothing might attract men, but the sound of conflict and fighting runs a real man away.

Mothers arguing with children

A young boy loves to be around his mother early in life because her words are ear candy that his heart desires, but watch his face when his mother uses negative words or argues with him. He will look confused and seemingly can't wait to escape the room. If this happens frequently, the young boy will find ways to distance himself from his mother and even from the house.

His actions prove that God has placed a deep desire in a man's heart to hear the right Sound from an early age.

If you ask a young boy or a man to explain how he feels about negative words from his mother, he will usually say that his mother argues with him or complains about what he does. He can't articulate the fact that his ears and heart are disturbed by the sound of those interactions.

It is proper and necessary for fathers and mothers to instruct their children, but mothers and fathers relate differently to their children. Sons can receive hardness from their fathers but need a softer sound from their mothers.

Many women are saddled with the responsibility of raising sons without the help of an on-site father. These women have to be both father and mother to their children. However, a son still needs to hear affirming sounds from his mother along with compliments and gratitude for the things that he does right. Then when she has to instruct and reprove him, he will receive it much better.

A husband doesn't like the sound of his wife arguing with the children. It is like fingernails on a chalkboard to him. Most men can't explain why it bothers them, so women keep bringing their anger issues to the men, using the same tone they used on the children. When he gives her this glazed over *I'm-trying-to-endure-this* look or tries to change the subject, she will say he isn't listening, and she's right. She never thinks about *why* he isn't listening. He wants her to give him *The Sound of Silence* or a pleasing sound that is attractive to his ears and moves his heart.

Complaining

"A continual dropping in a very rainy day and a contentious woman are alike."
—*Proverbs 27:15*

A man doesn't like hearing you complain. Complaining is the sister of arguing and can be nearly as destructive. Complaining is like someone nailing a pin through his eardrum. A woman should do her best to minimize complaining around her man. She should use *The Sound of Silence* instead.

Complaining is the opposite of gratitude. No one receives well an ungrateful person. A man will resist you when he feels you are taking actions that are only for your own good and not for his good. He will do everything in his ability to tune you out. He may love to spoil you, but when you seem self-spoiled, he hates that. He will ignore you. Don't allow those thoughts to surface in his mind.

Once he determines that you have stopped complaining and made a lifestyle change, then stayed the course, your relationship will improve as he sees that you have a new way of communicating and. His tone and demeanor will adjust to match your new way of relating to him. "A soft answer turns away wrath," the Scripture says (Proverbs 15:1 ESV). Now he is responding as a man should.

Comparing Him to Other Men

One thing a man hates more than anything else is being compared to other men. At all times there is a silent competition taking place between men and each one believes he has the upper hand, especially where his woman is concerned!

For this reason a man gets uncomfortable when meeting your old boyfriend or former mate. He immediately pictures you with this person and starts to compare himself with the other man.

You've seen this portrayed in the movies when the current boyfriend or husband isn't as put together as the past boyfriend or husband. Writers use the awkwardness for comic relief in the film, but it isn't funny in real life. Since men don't share their feelings, he could carry around an encounter like that for days.

I've talked with men who didn't like seeing an ex-girlfriend in the company of her current companion, even if he has had no recent contact. This may be a new revelation to many women, but it is genuine in the hearts of men.

Use *The Sound of Silence* instead of telling your man that a former boyfriend or your friend's husband does this or that better than he does. Even if it is true, you will have cut him deeply.

Never make this statement: "I wish you were like _____ " (another man). Don't even compare him to your father, because he is another man and qualifies as silent competition.

A man thinks a woman is pushy or bossy when she tells him to act like another man. He will resist her and do the opposite of what she wants, not only to be different but also to win the competition against another man. In his mind, where the other man is weak, he is strong. He is his own man.

Criticizing Him to Your Family

Women need to exalt the men in their lives to their families, not criticize them. My wife discovered early in our marriage she couldn't share her marital issues with me with her mother and sisters. After we had mended the fence, the family was still upset as though the offense was against them.

Instead of complaining to your family, use *The Sound of Silence* with them. Keep disagreements private between you and your husband and uplift him to family and friends.

Warning to Women in the Workplace

Science has proven that a chemical reaction takes place in a man's brain when he looks into the eyes of a woman. His reaction can be compared to the rush a person gets from using drugs. For this reason, I've instructed my daughters and the women in my church to always guard their eyes unless they are looking into the eyes of their husband or fiancé only. It is imperative for you to be careful in the workplace. If you speak to a man with The Sound that you use with your fiancé or your husband, he might read into it that you are interested in him. That is how much a man hungers for The Sound. This is especially true for a man with a negative-speaking woman in his life. Men who always hear a woman speaking negative words desperately needs to hear the positive words of a woman who understands *The Sound.*

No One Can Compare to My Man!

Instead of comparing your man to others, make him feel that no other man in this entire world can compare to him. Look into his eyes with a smile to show your satisfaction. Learn to employ eye contact with consistent smiles for the man in your life! Enjoy watching his chest inflate like Superman when you look into his eyes and smile!

It is always right to tell your man how much he means to you just the way he is, without sounding awkward or giving him the impression that you want something in return. A woman can destroy her entire efforts by wanting too much too fast. What you receive in return compared to what you are giving could be very little, but the transformation that takes place in you by speaking the right words will give you the greater gain.

For the sake of clarity, I am not advocating that you keep quiet about abuse. No abuse has any place in a relationship and family/friends should know about it if you have a problem. Spousal abuse is dangerous and must be revealed and dealt with severely!

However, life is full of common human conflicts and disagreements. Give those *The Sound of Silence.*

"Remember not only to say the right thing in the right place, but far more difficult still, to leave unsaid the wrong thing at the tempting moment."

—*Benjamin Franklin*

NOTES

The climax of seduction is to give the illusion that you're not trying to seduce.

—*Mathias Malzieu*

Chapter 8. The Sound of Seduction

Chapter 8

The Sound of Seduction

"With her much fair speech she caused him to yield, with the flattering of her lips she forced him."
—*Proverbs 7:21*

You might be asking the question, "Does making the proper sound really work?" Consider this example. Men can be completely fooled by a sexual chat service that they call on the phone to hear a woman making sounds of passion. Those sounds could come from an old woman sitting in an office reading a book while she makes the sounds. Meanwhile, the man is running over with excitement from thinking he is hearing the sound of passion and pleasure.

When I teach the principle of *The Sound* in men's meetings, they shake their heads up and down in affirmation. I make the argument that pornography is watched more for the sound than the images. Many different types of women do pornography, but after awhile there is nothing new to see so why do men keep watching? It is because of the sound! A man gets excited when he hears the sound of pleasure coming from a woman, even if she is making it for someone else in a movie. He is even excited when he hears the sound when it has nothing to do with sex.

Warnings from the Bible

The Bible gives examples and warnings about women who move men's hearts seductively and cause them to let down their guard down and do forbidden things.

Solomon writes in several Proverbs about women who use their words to entice a man into the house to engage in sexual intercourse. *The Sound of Seduction* is the way she speaks that makes him too weak to resist her enticements. This is one example from Proverbs that describes the destruction that results.

> *"For the lips of a strange woman drop as an honeycomb, and her mouth is smoother than oil: But her end is bitter as wormwood, sharp as a two-edged sword. Her feet go down to death; her steps take hold on hell. Lest thou shouldest ponder the path of life, her ways are moveable, that thou canst not know them."*
> —*Proverbs 5:3-6*

Samson yielded to *The Sound of Seduction*

Samson was the strongest man alive, but when he heard *The Sound of Seduction* from Delilah he told her his greatest secret. She knew how to get what she wanted.

Most people have heard the story about Samson and Delilah, but she was actually the second woman in Samson's life.

Samson's first woman

First, Samson wanted to marry another Philistine woman. The Bible doesn't give the woman's name. All we know about her is that she was pretty and she lived in Timnath.

According to Jewish marital laws, Samson was forbidden to marry outside of his culture, but when his parents couldn't change his mind about marrying a Philistine woman, they agreed to arrange the marriage.

On the way to Timnath to see this woman, Samson was confronted by a lion. The Bible says the Spirit of the Lord came upon him and gave him supernatural strength. He killed it with ease, using his bare hands, but Samson kept this event a secret.

His meeting with the young woman went well, and the Bible says, "She pleased him!" When he returned to see her again, he passed the lion carcass and saw that it was now full of bees that had produced honey. He ate some of the bees' honey and took some to give to his parents, but he didn't tell them where he got it.

During the seven-day feast to celebrate his marriage, Samson put forth a riddle to the men about the lion and the honey. He promised them clothing if they could solve the riddle in three days. When the men could not solve the riddle, they went to the new wife and demanded that she find out the answer. They told her if she refused they would murder her entire family. When she asked Samson to tell her, he wouldn't reveal his secret so she started crying and wouldn't stop until she broke him down.

Overtaken by *The Sound of Seduction*, Samson told his new wife the meaning of the riddle and she revealed the mystery to the Philistines. When Samson found out that they had used his new bride to manipulate him, he ended the marriage. This woman had manipulated Samson, and no man likes manipulation.

Delilah Turns Up the Heat

Samson then met his infamous Philistine lover, Delilah. She also pleased him, but she turned up the heat. Now the Philistines wanted to know the source of Samson's tremendous strength and how to defeat him. Delilah didn't use crying to manipulate him. She told Samson how good he would make her feel if he revealed the source of his strength. For a long time, he resisted her, but even a man with supernatural strength can't beat *The Sound of Seduction* when it comes from an expert woman.

Finally, Samson told her that he must never cut his hair and she revealed his secret to the Philistine leaders. They told her to cut his hair while he slept and then they captured him.

Now if Samson with all of his strength couldn't handle a woman who spoke to him in just the right way, then how do you think The Sound will affect the common everyday man? Samson fell for it twice, and both times it was used against him. When you use *The Sound*, you will use it to benefit your man and you.

Danger of a Marriage Without *The Sound*

Sometimes a relationship between a man and a woman that has made it past the five-year mark will decline into an old and predictable zone. Both persons are locked into regular, everyday routines that drain all of the excitement. Even if the man doesn't hear *The Sound* at home, he still craves it so he seeks it somewhere else. It doesn't always go as far as an affair or inappropriate communication with another woman, but sometimes it does.

Men who don't hear *The Sound* at home may hear a friendly woman at a store, a woman who recognizes his abilities at work, or a waitress who makes a big deal about a tip he gave her. His need and desire to hear *The Sound* is fulfilled by someone other than his wife.

What Call Girls Understand

When the popular and notorious dating hookup site Ashley Madison was hacked a few years ago, hundreds of Christian leaders had the covers rolled back and their secret lives were exposed because they had profiles on the site. Many were married men in long-standing relationships with their wives.

How did Christian men become so excited about meeting another woman for a potential affair while at the same time losing their excitement about loving their wives? The easy answer is that they were just dogs! I agree that an ingredient of dog-like behavior accompanies this activity. But that is not all.

A woman who sells her body or seeks an affair understands how to flirt with a man using *The Sound of Seduction*. To get what she desires, she speaks to him in a seductive, playful voice. She does everything in her power to make him comfortable. She makes no requirements like those his wife expects of him at home. He allows himself to get at ease. He is excited about trying to please this woman and to hear the sound of her pleasure.

These women are not genuinely interested in the men. They are skilled at using *The Sound of Seduction* to get men to give them what they want.

In no way am I endorsing or legitimizing this illicit behavior. However, the mistress and call girl knows how to entice a man while making him feel like a man. The principles outlined in this book were not designed for the mistress and call girl but for the woman who wants her man to cleave to her and desire her. A wife should always provide *The Sound That He Listens For*.

The Sound of Jezebel's Influence

Much is said about Jezebel today concerning her influence over her husband King Ahab. It is even referred to as the spirit of Jezebel, but few if any leaders investigate why she had this type of influence. The secret is in *The Sound*.

Jezebel's husband Ahab was clearly a wicked man in the sight of God. His wife was a pagan prostitute who wanted to introduce pagan worship into the kingdom of Israel. Their intriguing story can be found in the Bible in the books of First and Second Kings.

Jezebel was wicked and she was an expert in using *The Sound of Seduction*. Using her influence, she convinced King Ahab to confiscate land, commit murder, and rebel against God.

However, God was not influenced by Jezebel. God used Elijah the prophet to bring His judgment on Ahab's reign. Single-handedly, Elijah faced down 450 prophets of Baal who served under her direct covering, defeated them, and had them all killed.

Jezebel's dominating brought her death

However, Jezebel was not finished yet. She sent Elijah a terrifying message that he faced the same fate as her prophets and he would die in 24 hours. When this great prophet heard *The Sound of Jezebel's Influence*, he was so intimidated that he ran away. Elijah didn't run from men, including King Ahab, but this one woman had him running for his life and hiding in a cave.

Men can become intimidated and run away in fear when they hear *The Sound of Jezebel's Influence*. We usually deal with Jezebel's sexual exploits, her strong will, and her pagan worship, and those things are important. However, we must never overlook the way she used *The Sound of Jezebel's Influence* to dominate two powerful men—a king and a prophet.

The spirit of Jezebel causes men to run and hide. Even today, some women pattern their lives after this wicked queen, calling her courageous and misunderstood. However, God didn't allow Jezebel to continue to live in her day and He will not allow the spirit of Jezebel to live in this day, either.

Beware of celebrating someone whom God marks as evil.

The Sound of Seduction from Solomon's Wives

Throughout this book, quotes from King Solomon's proverbs have been used that indicate the depth of his study of women. Solomon had more than 1,000 wives and concubines. He wrote about the importance of women but also about their potential negative effects on men, including him. He instructed men to watch for and resist The Sound of Seduction at all costs.

Solomon was one of the wisest and wealthiest men who ever lived. He was chosen as king and given the right to complete the temple that his father David had desired to build for the Lord. When God asked what Solomon wanted from Him, he requested wisdom and knowledge to lead the people. This pleased God so much that He granted Solomon's request and gave him even more.

"And God said to Solomon, Because this was in thine heart, and thou hast not asked riches, wealth, or honour, nor the life of thine enemies, neither yet hast asked long life; but hast asked wisdom and knowledge for thyself, that thou mayest judge my people, over whom I have made thee king: Wisdom and knowledge is granted unto thee; and I will give thee riches, and

wealth, and honour, such as none of the kings have had that have been before thee, neither shall there any after thee have the like. —2 Chronicles 1:11-12

Not much is said about the women in Solomon's life, but his writings in the Bible reveal his experiences. It is clear that these women seduced him away from God and persuaded him to serve other gods. Solomon studied women to better understand their positive and negative influence over men, but his wealth and wisdom were no match for *The Sound of Seduction.*

NOTES

If you want to become fully mature in the Lord, you must learn to love truth. Otherwise, you will always leave open a door of deception for the enemy to take what is meant to be yours.

—Joyce Meyer

CHAPTER 9. THE SOUND OF DECEPTION

Chapter 9
The Sound of Deception

Be real at all times. Men dislike fake things. They can easily detect a counterfeit laugh mainly because a laugh includes more than sound. Your eyes are involved as well. Watch a person who tells a joke; they will look in the faces of the people laughing to see if its real.

Don't tell him that something he is doing is excellent if you don't believe it! He will know that you are not real. Find those things where you can sincerely express to him your gratitude and joy. Real works, fake hurts!

Fake Listening

This flaw is one of the main issues women discuss when highlighting their men and relationships. He doesn't listen!

However, if truth be told he isn't alone in this department. A woman just has a better ability to hide the fact she isn't listening because her brain works differently.

A woman can communicate from both sides of her brain at the same time. The man can use only one side of his brain at a time. That makes it difficult for him to focus on two things at the same time. This is the reason men focus on the one thing they are doing as though nothing else in the world matters. When you allow him to shut out distractions of all types, he can complete his tasks.

When a man wants to talk, he approaches the talk with the belief that his woman can stay focused in the same way he can. He expects her undivided attention. However, since a woman has difficulty focusing on only one thing, her mind can travel to many places while he is talking. She thinks about changing the carpet, picking up the children, meeting her girlfriends later and what to wear. When he detects this, he will accuse her of not listening.

When she is able to repeat back everything he said, he will think she was actually listening, but she wasn't listening!

Be honest! Say to him, "Can you repeat that? My mind wandered." Work on staying focused by making comments and asking questions for further understanding as he talks. Most men enjoy a woman's active listening. Just remember, please don't offer opinions or instructions if you are not asked. Show excitement without concern. You will be able to come back later and voice your concerns and opinions, but at first just listen. If he asks what you think, ask for some time to think about it.

Just don't act like you are listening when you are not!

Fake Happiness

Too many women in the world and especially in the church have learned to fake happiness. My caution to women in our meetings is to never make a man believe they are happy, excited, or grateful for something unless they mean it! The man will take a mental note of this approval and purchase that item or perform in that way over and over again.

The one thing that I'm entirely clear about is the fact that God created the woman after the man so that she would be truly happy and have no needs. She would experience a joyful life. Jesus came to restore us to the place where we were before the point of the Fall. He can take us back to those beginnings when the Godhead created humanity.

Tell him the truth about what you want

This will again get me in trouble with my fellow male counterparts. Even though most men won't tell this, the fact is that a man wants to know a woman's true desires. He doesn't want to figure out what she wants. Moreover, he is willing and ready to provide for her every wish! Most men really want to make the women in their lives happy and will use a laser-like focus to accomplish that task. Tell him how to do this and show true happiness, then sit back and reap the benefits.

NOTES

_____

_____

_____

_____

_____

_____

_____

_____

The ear is the avenue to the heart.

—Voltaire

Chapter 10

The Sound That He Listens For

"A good wife is her husband's pride and joy.
—*Proverbs 12:4*

"He who finds a wife finds what is good and receives favor from the LORD."
—*Proverbs 18:22*

A glimpse at the sexual experience reveals principles that form the foundation of *The Sound That He Listens For*.

When a husband and wife engage in intercourse, the woman can make sounds of passion that completely excite the man. It doesn't work the same when the man makes all types of sounds. Therefore, it is clear that the ears of a man can be a way to his heart. The main key in this book is learning how to take the sounds of passion outside of the bedroom into everyday life.

To demonstrate *The Sound* in my *The True Value of a Woman* meetings, I project a picture of puppies on the screen and all of the women say, *"Oooh,"* without being prompted. Then I project a picture of a newborn baby on the screen and their sound changes to *"Ahhh,"* but the attitude is the same.

Their reaction to these images provides me with the opportunity to tell them that they may know how to make *The Sound*, but they might not know when or for whom to make it.

The True Value of a Woman is a movement that is designed to bring women back to their God-ordained purpose so that a man and woman can again rule and reign with Christ and enjoy a small part of heaven while on earth. I believe that women who understand and use *The Sound* as it has been described in this book will help shift the interaction between men and women to a new level of joy that they have never experienced before.

Why have marriage relationships suffered, even among Christians? Because most women have never heard how much their communications affect men so they never learn the communication skills to save and enhance their relationships.

Fragile. Do Not Break.

Men are powerful creatures, but they break easily. A good wife can not only keep him from breaking but also build him up into the man that God created him to be.

Men are designed and wired by God to respond positively to the persuasive and grateful words of a woman. However, because men showcase their strength, women miss the fact that men are breakable and that the woman is often the one responsible for breaking him down with her wrong words or attitudes.

Once a woman accepts her responsibilities, restoration will come. Restoration begins with her attitude of repentance and her willingness to change.

The Sound of Encouragement

Many women believe it is their duty to tell the men in their lives what to do, to tell them what they are doing wrong and when they are being complete idiots. But doing this will completely backfire in most cases. I would agree that there are areas where a man needs a woman's help and instruction, but the way you tell him will create the change. He needs encouragement, too.

Encourage him first before you give him instructions about something you want him to do or tell him your desires. Correction from the wrong spirit without saying anything positive will provoke an argument or the man will shut down and have nothing else to say. This can cause another confrontation when the woman tries to get him to explain why he is quiet. All of this could have been avoided with *The Sound of Silence*. A woman wise and secure enough in herself does not need to have someone tell her she was right. She knows when to be silent and to leave him alone.

Most men will position themselves to make it appear that they don't need to be encouraged because they think people who need constant compliments and encouragement can be quite annoying. However, don't let that distract you. He does need encouragement, especially from the woman in his life.

> *"She openeth her mouth with wisdom; and in her tongue is the law of kindness."*
> *—Proverbs 31:25*

Men love to hear you tell them they have done a great job. The more you encourage a man, the better he will seek to become better. Your encouragement tells him he is pleasing you. Believe it or not, he lives to please you.

Use Your Secret Sauce

You can learn something about approaching a man from what the Bible says about approaching God in prayer. It says when you communicate with God, give Him thanks, don't just recite a list of requests. Acknowledge God from a position of respect and honor and gratitude. The same principle applies to a man.

When you make a list of things you want your man to do, do you focus on how much it blesses you when he does things for you? Or maybe you focus on a new list of things you want him to do and complain about all the things he did wrong the last time or never did at all. A relationship doesn't taste very good when one or the other person is always bitter like that.

Any relationship tastes better when you use the secret sauce of gratitude.

When you are approaching prayer, you should make a running list of how good God has been to you in the past. List things you are thankful for. Approach God with the right sound.

The same applies to the men in your life. Approach them with the right sound, *The Sound That He Listens For*. Before you list all the things he did wrong or didn't do the last time, ask yourself, "Does he ever do anything right? What does he *always* do right?" Then make a point of telling him and giving him your thanks. That is not only common sense, it also follows the biblical model of Christ and the Church, which is the Bride of Christ.

The Bible says a wife should relate to her husband as the Church relates to Christ.

> *"For the husband is the head of the wife, even as Christ is the head of the church: and he is the saviour of the body. Therefore as the church is subject unto Christ, so let the wives be to their own husbands in every thing."*
> —*Ephesians 5:23-24*

As Christians, we make requests to God in prayer with an added ingredient—the secret sauce of thanksgiving.

Look at this passage about prayer from the book of Philippians and notice the phrase *"with thanksgiving."*

> *"Be careful for nothing; but in everything by prayer and supplication **with thanksgiving** let your requests be made known unto God."*
> —Philippians 4:6

The Apostle Paul is instructing Christ's Bride how to move the heart of our Husband and King—God. The same principle works for the woman who wants to move the heart of her husband.

The secret sauce of thanksgiving shows God that you are not a taker. You appreciate what He has given to you. The same applies to *The Sound* of gratitude toward your man. A woman who seasons words to her husband with the secret sauce of gratitude and thanksgiving can reopen life's locked doors. Thanksgiving combined with gratefulness is the sauce that makes everything taste so much better.

When a woman acknowledges her husband's protection and provision with heartfelt gratefulness, she has hit a sweet spot. Now he has become her hero, a knight in shining armor, or any other description you know that shows respect and honor.

When a woman tells a man about the things that make her happy and give her pleasure, it benefits *the woman*, but saying "Thank you" benefits *the man*. Saying thank you to a man and expressing joy for the things he has done for you and how well he has done them causes him to prance around like a young rooster.

Praise for the Woman Who Empowers a Man

Proverbs 31 has long been the place to find the description of an empowering woman who is called virtuous. A woman should study these verses and make them a vital part of her life!

10. Who can find a virtuous woman? for her price is far above rubies.

11. The heart of her husband doth safely trust in her, so that he shall have no need of spoil.

12. She will do him good and not evil all the days of her life.

13. She seeketh wool, and flax, and worketh willingly with her hands.

14. She is like the merchants' ships; she bringeth her food from afar.

15. She riseth also while it is yet night, and giveth meat to her household, and a portion to her maidens.

16. She considereth a field, and buyeth it: with the fruit of her hands she planteth a vineyard.

17. She girdeth her loins with strength, and strengtheneth her arms.

18. She perceiveth that her merchandise is good: her candle goeth not out by night.

19. She layeth her hands to the spindle, and her hands hold the distaff.

20. She stretcheth out her hand to the poor; yea, she reacheth forth her hands to the needy.

21. She is not afraid of the snow for her household: for all her household are clothed with scarlet.

22. She maketh herself coverings of tapestry; her clothing is silk and purple.

23. She maketh fine linen, and selleth it; and delivereth girdles unto the merchant.

24. Strength and honour are her clothing; and she shall rejoice in time to come.

25. She openeth her mouth with wisdom; and in her tongue is the law of kindness.

26. She looketh well to the ways of her household, and eateth not the bread of idleness.

27. Her children arise up, and call her blessed; her husband also, and he praiseth her.

28. Many daughters have done virtuously, but thou excellest them all.

29. Favour is deceitful, and beauty is vain: but a woman that feareth the LORD, she shall be praised.

30. Give her of the fruit of her hands; and let her own works praise her in the gates.

31. Her husband is known in the gates, when he sitteth among the elders of the land.

The Sound of Empowerment

I once saw an advertisement that said, "Let us make you feel like a king!" When I saw that, I responded out loud, "That position is filled in my life!" I already feel like a king because my wife understands *The Sound.*

A man becomes manlier when the woman in his life uses The Sound in ways that empower him. Just by being the women God that designed them to be, women can help their fathers, husbands, sons and other men in their lives.

How many men do you know who would react the same way I did *when I heard The Sound*?

Would the man in your life react that way?

What will you now change based on reading this book?

NOTES

I don't do a lot of looking back; I tend to look ahead.

—Marie Helvin

Chapter 11. I'm Never Going Back

Chapter 11
I'm Never Going Back

"And Adam said, This is now bone of my bones, and flesh of my flesh: she shall be called Woman, because she was taken out of Man. Therefore shall a man leave his father and his mother, and shall cleave unto his wife: and they shall be one flesh."
—Genesis 2:23-24

When Adam met the wife that God had given him, he gave us the Bible's first definition of marriage (above), which included the commitment to "cleave."

Cleaving means a man views the woman as himself and not as a separate being. Therefore, he will nourish, cherish and love her in the same way he would do those things for himself. His thoughts and actions have his wife's best interest at the center.

The Sound reminds him of God's design and a man's responsibility to cleave to his wife. In essence, *The Sound* causes masculinity in men to increase.

Because men respond to *The Sound* and those principles empower them to be better men, it would appear that they are the beneficiary. The real beneficiary of *The Sound* is Women!

God knew what He was doing when He created a woman in the way and at the time that He did it. The woman already had a man waiting for her and everything was in place for her to live free of worry and care.

Cleaving is something that husbands do

Cleaving to the woman is something for the husband to do, and it is a big deal. Women need to know their men desire them. However, I don't know if most women could handle a cleaving man. Notice I didn't say, clingy man! There is a big difference.

The Apostle Paul clarified the Genesis passage when he was writing to the Ephesians. He instructed fallen men to remember and understand what cleaving entails.

> *"So ought men to love their wives as their own bodies. He that loveth his wife loveth himself. For no man ever yet hated his own flesh; but nourisheth and cherisheth it, even as the Lord the church: For we are members of his body, of his flesh, and of his bones. For this cause shall a man leave his father and mother, and shall be joined unto his wife, and they two shall be one flesh."*
> *—Ephesians 5:28-31*

There is no way possible to have a 50 percent divorce rate when men are cleaving to their wives.

In the beginning, the woman was united as one with the man. Together they functioned as overseers of the earth and everything in it. The fallen nature has not only separated man and woman from God but also separated man and woman from one another. I believe that women suffer more from this modern tendency for separation than men do.

God designed the man to fulfill all of the woman's desires and his disobedience in the Garden changed a great deal, but the Fall didn't change a man's ear/heart connection.

The time has come for women to again enjoy their God-designed position and receive true love from their men. It is time to be happy!

Although the proper use of *The Sound* has so much power, I have found that many women attending our conferences have no idea how to use it or how to master this powerful tool. Women would interrupt my teaching by calling out loud in the middle of the meeting to ask for help learning the principles!

After further investigation, we discovered that their inability to understand and apply the principle of *The Sound* and function naturally had a great deal to do with other women in their lives. Their mothers, grandmothers, aunts and other older women had taught them wrong concepts about how to get and keep a man's attention and cooperation.

Many times the women urgently asking questions in our conferences were unmarried and wanted to understand the principles better before engaging in a relationship or marriage. These women can still use *The Sound* because the man doesn't need a romantic connection to benefit. He only needs to be a man.

Some women think they are already functioning according to this principle and blame their men for refusing to respond right or behave right. However, he may be looking and listening for the right things before he reacts and many times he can't articulate what he wants to see before he responds.

Major frustrations can take root if she has done what's outlined in this book yet there is no apparent change coming from the man. He is still not meeting her needs or responding to the ways she has changed

I intend to prepare women for possible pitfalls they could face in the process of their change and the implementation of *The Sound*. Below are some of the responses you may see *when he hears The Sound.*

He May Respond Negatively When He First Hears *The Sound*

Men are creatures of habit. Therefore, when you begin to implement the principles of *The Sound* your man may experience a wide range of emotions. If you are not prepared to handle them, his attitude might sabotage your efforts.

Let me assure you that regardless of the outward evidence, *when he hears The Sound* he will notice, but he may become stubborn. In the early stages, your efforts might seem to be fruitless. Stay the course.

Below are some approaches that you can use to react to his responses *when he hears The Sound*. They are not a quick fix by any means, but they will pay off in the long run. Reading *The True Value of a Woman* book will help you understand your value in God while waiting for your man to appreciate your worth.

Confusion

One of the first responses a woman may see in her man when she begins to use *The Sound* is his complete confusion! You may recall from Chapter 1 how I responded with shock to my wife Joanndra when she completely changed her tone toward me in the midst of a developing argument.

The man who never hears *The Sound* has actually adjusted to the negative ways that his wife or other women around him respond in various life situations. He may not like all of their actions and responses, but he has found ways to deal with them, from ignoring them to starting an argument himself. He has even learned to be comfortable when things get explosive, because at least it is predictable!

When his wife or another woman suddenly stops responding in the way he expects or starts speaking to him according to the principles of *The Sound*, he may feel defenseless. There are reports of men who tried to pick an argument, fight back, or bait her so that she would respond in a way that was familiar.

Here are some descriptions of confusion that you may see:

- Disorder; upheaval; tumult; chaos
- The army retreated in confusion
- Lack of clearness or distinctness
- Perplexity; bewilderment
- Embarrassment or abashment
- Psychiatry, a disturbed mental state; disorientation
- Archaic—defeat, overthrow, or ruin

When a woman understands that her change and use of *The Sound* is the reason for the man's confusion and even his attacks, it will be easier for her to stay the course.

Lots of questions

He may have simple questions, spoken and unspoken:

"What happened to you?"

"Where is the woman I know?"

"What did you do with my wife, mother, sister or girlfriend?"

If the man is able to verbalize one or more of these questions, the woman has received a wonderful blessing. When this happens, she can use his questions to strengthen her position. She might say something like this:

"I realize how special you are and how much I love you, and I just want to show you in the way we interact."

"I've awakened to the fact that we aren't as unified as we should be and it has a great deal to do with my actions or reactions."

These responses may deepen his confusion, but that isn't a bad thing. Many times when the mind doesn't understand something it becomes willing to learn.

From this point on, it is important to realize that he will be watching you like a hawk looking for prey. The prey he is looking for, in this case, is your failure! It is imperative that you stay consistent. If you fail, be quick to repent and move forward again.

Resistance

Resistance. The act or power of resisting, opposing, or withstanding. The opposition offered by one thing, force, etc., to another.

Another response you may see is total resistance to your change and your new attitudes. In the minds of some men, a change this significant in your words and deeds looks like manipulation. One thing a man hates is when he believes a woman is trying to manipulate him.

Sometimes he will allow you to manipulate him if he thinks it is to his advantage, but in most cases if a man smells the scent of manipulation, he will resist all of a woman's efforts. Since this new attitude and position have taken him by surprise and he has never been accustomed to seeing you act like this, he may go into a strictly defensive posture.

Compliance

The act of conforming, acquiescing or yielding.

A tendency to yield readily to others, especially in a weak and subservient way. Conformity; accordance: cooperation or obedience.

Once the man has moved past the confused and resistance stages, he may seem to become more compliant. This experience may seem pleasurable to you, but you haven't seen anything yet. When he seems to be settling into this new way of living and communicating, it is time for you to step up the game plan.

Renewing Your Mind and Never Going Back

"I beseech you therefore, brethren, by the mercies of God, that ye present your bodies a living sacrifice, holy, acceptable unto God, which is your reasonable service."

"And be not conformed to this world: but be ye transformed by the renewing of your mind, that ye may prove what is that good, and acceptable, and perfect, will of God."
—Romans 12:1-2

If the women in your family resist your change when you share with them what I have just told you about the effectiveness of *The Sound*, stand your ground. You have renewed your mind. You are never going back. You have a new understanding of your relationship with the men in your life and you have chosen the principles of *The Sound*.

If you are married, you have offered your life to God and to your husband. It may have been difficult for you to change, but your family can benefit from what you have learned as well as you. You can become their teacher based on Scripture.

NOTES

Chapter 12. Bring on the Joy

Joy is the serious business of Heaven
—C.S. Lewis

Chapter 12
Bring on the Joy!

*Joy—"the emotion of great delight or
happiness caused by something exceptionally
good or satisfying; keen pleasure; elation . . .
a source or cause of intense pleasure or
delight; something or someone greatly valued
or appreciated . . . the expression or display of
glad feeling; festive gaiety . . . a state of
happiness or felicity" (dictionary.com)*

The women's movement with a focus.

Women and the women's movement have a
unique opportunity to be at the center of a new
narrative and national conversation about men and
women by focusing on the development of positive
male role models for future generations.

When women begin to focus on developing
better men, dads, husbands, boyfriends, and sons, it
will not come at the expense of giving rightful
attention to women's rights and equality. It will
expand those benefits and actually increase them.

This is my challenge to you. Lay a new
foundation for a hopeful and positive future for both
men and women. You cannot lay a foundation for
support, guidance and respect for men if you
maintain your focus on confronting them with
systematic attacks on their masculinity. Instead,

acknowledge that men are in crisis but you have the solutions.

I believe that this will bring hope for a new kingdom.

Competition Didn't Come with Creation

Throughout this book, I have outlined how women can receive direct benefits when they allow men to think and act like men. The Bible says we live in a world that the Apostle Paul described as "neither male nor female." Jesus came to restore our world with man and woman at the center of His restoration, walking in authority and blessings together, just as they were at the beginning of creation.

In the beginning of creation, the woman was one with the man and they functioned together as overseers of the earth and all that is in it. Competition between men and women did not exist in God's original design.

The church world has missed this reality by focusing only on the time of salvation instead of looking back to the time of creation and even before, to the place of true beginnings.

Jesus redeemed us not only back to the Fall but also back before the Fall when the Godhead originally determined to create mankind.

Woman Was Created Without Needs

In the creation account, the man was created first. This was not because he was better than the woman but so that he would be in position to worship God and provide for the woman before she came!

God created the woman from the side of the man, and she has absolutely no needs. The first man was clear about this. Even without instructions from God, he knew that she was his very essence—Bone of His Bones and Flesh of His Flesh! She was created *from* him to join *with* him in worshipping God and enjoying all the divine blessings that God provided.

It is clear that God created the woman to experience more pleasure than the man and he was designed to provide it. In my book *The True Value of a Woman* I discussed the fact that a woman is the only creature given an organ designed for the sole purpose of pleasure. Why would God create such an organ unless she had the purpose of living her life with the experience of joy and pleasure forever?

Bring On the Joy!

I want women to return to the place where they are so connected to their men that they can say, "Bring on the joy!"

Since I live with a wife and five daughters, that has helped me to understand how important happiness is to women. The quote that says "When Momma's not happy, no one is happy" is a factual statement. Therefore, I do my best to keep my wife happy. My daughters have watched this happen all of their lives and they understand that this is the way it is supposed to be.

I wrote this book because the time has come again for women to enjoy their God-designed position and receive true love from their men. Too many women in the world, and especially in the church, have to fake their happiness. Too many women proclaim that they don't need a man or that men are predators.

It is time for a change! Even though some men have taken advantage of women and have abused them, I believe that the majority of men still want to please the women in their lives.

God gave women amazing power. He did not give women this power to overthrow men but to strengthen and encourage them. Their power baffles the mind!

Some women who have had this power all along did not know how to use it until they read this book. Other women already knew that their men responded to them easily but they could not explain it until they found the answers in this book. It has confirmed their lives.

No matter what camp you are in, please understand this—new life begins when a woman understands how to move a man's heart through his ears!

NOTES

About the Author

Bishop Larry A. Jackson is the founding senior pastor of Bethel Outreach International Church, Charlotte, NC. He is also the founder of Frontliners Ministries which includes the Breastplate Prayer Movement International; www.breatplateprayer.org and The True Value of a Woman Movement; www.truevalueofawoman.com. He is the author of several books, including *One Degree of Change, The True Value of a Woman, The Power is in the Closet, Knowing God by the Numbers, Numbered with the Transgressors, Guilt Free Living,* and *Beyond Reconciliation.*

55484114R00080

Made in the USA
Columbia, SC
17 April 2019